"E-Z Te
took me
through
knew it,
do my grandkids. Everyone has to do
this...it's just so fun!!"
-          -Dan, Retired & Grandpa of twins

In this charming book, the author opens
a door into a world that too many in
the 50+ age group find confusing, even
terrifying: texting. Step-by-step, Marti
reveals everything needed to participate
in this new wave of communication:
basic texting, a dictionary of words &
phrases, and helpful web addresses for
those wanting to go that extra texting
mile. Best of all, the author delivers
everything in a friendly, encouraging
voice. From turning on the cell phone to
actually creating and sending the text
message, she makes it seem just what it
has become: child's play!

:-)

We've all seen them: elementary school children, restaurant patrons, sometimes even drivers, all focused on that little cell phone and busily, often joyfully, punching out messages. What are they doing? Texting! While most of us are sending emails or leaving voice messages asking "Where are you?" there are fingers all over the world texting the native language's version of W r U ? In E-Z Text Messaging 4 Grandparents, the riddle is not only translated, the mystery is fully solved! In writing that is both precise and entertaining, Marti takes readers by the hand and guides us through the ins and outs of texting. From basic technique to a sometimes hilarious dictionary of words, phrases, and acronyms, with a bonus section of websites where we can learn even more about this communication phenomenon, everything is explained clearly, simply, and in a language perhaps too elementary for our children, but absolutely spot-on for anyone over fifty!

If you want to jump on the 21st century's communication bandwagon, you must learn how to text. Your friends are doing it, your children and grandchildren are doing it, even your business associates are texting. Those who can't speak 'texting' have their FC (fingers crossed) that they'll get by.

What seems like a mysterious jumble of letters and numbers is magically explained in E-Z Text Messaging 4 Grandparents. And it is done clearly, humorously, and with the final goal being successful cell phone texting. Marti guides her readers through all the phases of texting, including basic techniques, a riotous dictionary of words & phrases, even a section listing websites if you want to go beyond basics. Emails are fine, if you are sitting at your desk, but what happens when you're on the run? You text! And if you don't know how, you've found the perfect guide. You can do it!

"The very best thing about all of this is that you really, really can stay connected with your grandkids through text messaging. And, that's my true goal: keeping the generations connected."

--Valli Marti, Author

E-Z
TEXT
MESSAGING
4
GRANDPARENTS

(And, other 50+ ers)

Staying in touch

:-)

valli p. marti

vallipublishing company
norman ok
vallipub.com

Con Amor
Para Mi
Nieta y Mis Nietos,
Kaylee, Brodie, y Jack

E-Z
TEXT
MESSAGING
4
GRANDPARENTS

Welcome to E-Z Text Messaging 4 Grandparents! I am really glad you purchased this easy guide to texting. Your grandkids are going to be so impressed when they find out you can text message.

It's much easier than you can imagine. I was completely surprised that I could learn to do this. After I 'made' & sent my first message, I immediately wanted other Grandparents to be able to do this. Why? Because it was so much fun and such a special kind of connection with each of my grandchildren.

But, I didn't think I could

write a text-messaging 'basics'
that would help grandparents
because, when the idea came to
me, I had only written and sent
that one message.

Yet, my granddaughter,
Katie was so totally surprised
and awed to get a 'Good luck
tonight' message from her
Grammie on the day of her
ballet performance this year,
that I knew I had to try. I had
to share this with others.

I thought' "More of us
'older' folks should be able to
do this! It's our grand kids'
favorite way to communicate.
So why not let them know how

great they are!-- in a way that they can really relate to."

A couple of weeks after Katie's performance, I got brave & decided to try texting her again. I sent her another message with more words. I was practicing. Here's her reply (I loved this. It's still on my phone for re-reading),

"Wow! I'm impressed. You have potential to be a gr8 texter! XOXO, Katie"

She was nice to her Grammie & didn't use all texting lingo. She knows I'm a beginner. But... Did I feel good or what!!!!???!!!!! I felt like we had a new, secret kind of connection between us!

You can and will feel this great, too. I promise! In five minutes or less!

I wanted to share this feeling with others like myself, but I thought at first that I just didn't know enough. But, then, I realized that this was the perfect time to write an uncomplicated, keep-it-simple, beginning text-messaging guide for the 'grand' generation.

Because I'm just learning, I explain things that others take for granted. Things advanced texters assume or that seem obvious to them.

I'll bet you start getting responses today, because you're going to be sending your first message shortly.

So, as I said, I'm going to keep it short, simple & direct because that's how I learn new technology best.
SIMPLE...E-Z

So here we go......

Just so you'll know: This is a
3 PART GUIDE

1.   BASICS

**2.   WORDS &
PHRASES**

3.   WEB SITES: options
for more words & phrases,
for later

     So, let's start with a few
basics and then we'll create
your first message. You'll send

it shortly, in just a few minutes.
Surprised? Don't be.
Remember, I told you it would
take 5 minutes or less from the
time we start on your first
message.

Here's a **Head's-Up**

Most cell phone plans
include text messaging. Some
do not charge for this service
and some do.

You'll have to look on
your bill or call your cell phone
company to find out, if you
don't already know this. They
can tell you in just a couple of
minutes what your plan includes.

It's very inexpensive to

add even if your company does charge.

Most offer several options, including
* a simple, single charge for each message of about 160 characters or less – and, that's pretty long in text lingo
* monthly rates
* yearly rates

If you don't have this, just tell them you're a grand-parent, that you won't be sending a whole lot of messages, & you want the best possible deal.

Ask for a senior discount
-they might have one.

1. BASICS--
GETTING
STARTED

First, get your cell phone &
open it. Look at it.

KEY PAD: source of
letters, numbers, & symbols

> **Key pad summary:**
> 2, 3, 4, 5, 6, & 8   = 3
> alphabet letters each
>
> 7 & 9 = 4 alphabet letter
> each

It looks like this

C (clear)

1	**2** **a b c**	**3** **d e f**
4 **g h i**	**5** **j k l**	**6** **m n o**
7 **p q r s**	**8** **t u v**	**9** **w x y z**

So, if you punch key pad 2, 1x,

  you will get an 'a'

 if you punch key pad 2,
    2x,
    you will get a 'b'

 if you punch key pad 2,
    3x,
    you will get a 'c'

HINT: pausing after punches
    if you want the letter 'b',
    then punch key pad 2, 2x
    quickly.
Don't pause between punches.
But, if you do pause & end up
with the letter 'a',
    just punch the big 'C'

(clear) button that's up
above the key pad

& it will erase the letter.

SO, LET'S TRY IT!!

Say, for example, you wanted to
tell you grandchild that you
loved them, then here's what
you'd do:

A) **Open your phone**

punch the 'menu' button

Select 'messages'

(on my phone this looks like a
mail box)

Then select '**create new
message**'

Then select '**text
message**'

Now, look around at the various
displays on your phone for a
small bar or rectangle that
has something like:

AABB or **AaBb** or

123 or **T9Ab**

(On my phone it's in the upper right corner **of the screen**. On GrandPa's phone, it's on the lower left)

this bar tells you whether you will be entering text letters in all **Capitals,**
Capitals & Small letters
Numbers,
or some other combination

after you find this bar, look to see if there are **all letters on the bar**; if so, you're fine

if not, then punch the * key until you see all letters for now, it doesn't matter if it's all capitals or capitals & small letters

The * key is usually at the bottom of the key pad, just after the #9 key.

Hint: if the * key doesn't change this, then try the # or even both keys at the same time. This is not hard.

But texting will be frustrating if you don't have the AABB orAaBb combination selected.

Don't freak. If I did this without instructions, I know you can do it! **Everything after this is a piece of cake**.

B) Next comes writing the
message – which is what
this is all about

Let's make a text message to
one of your grandchildren that
says: **"I love you"**

In text lingo, 'I love you' is
written: **i luv u**

So, here we go > > > >
> > > > > > > > > > > > > > > > > >

i luv u

i = key pad 4, 3 quick punches

space = key pad #,   1 punch

l = key pad 5,   3 punches

u = key pad 8,   2 punches

v = key pad 8,   3 punches

space = key pad #,   1 punch

u = key pad 8,   2 punches

Wow!, you've done it !!   The
message is there.   Good work!
Now, all that's left is to send it.

C)   On your phone

select '**options**'

select '**send**':

there will be a window to enter the **cell phone # of your grandchild**

or

If you don't want to enter the phone number manually, you can select '**address book**' & then select you're your grandchild's phone # and click on that name

Hit 'send'

That's it!   A B C

CONGRATULATIONS !
! ! ! ! ! ! ! ! ! ! ! ! ! ! ! !

YOU HAVE ACTUALLY
CREATED
AND
SENT YOUR VERY FIRST
TEXT MESSAGE!

Amazed?   Well, after all, We
ARE the Grands & Greats of
the world!!

Now, all you have to do is
practice by sending more

messages. Or, you could even
create messages just for
practice & not send them.

In fact, let's try another.

A) Okay, open your
phone & go to 'text message'
'create message'

B) Hmmm, what shall we
say? How about **"See you
tonight."**

So, now think in
your head what that would be in
'text' lingo

Got it?   Right.
C   U   2nite

Let's type it:
Key pad 2,   punch 3x = c

Key pad #,   punch 1x = space

Key pad 8,   punch 2x = u

Key pad #,   punch 1x = space

Key pad 2,   punch 4x = 2

Key pad 6,   punch 2x = n

Key pad 4,   punch 3x = i

Key pad 8,   punch 1x = t

Key pad 3,   punch 2x = e

And, you've done it!
The message is there.

C) Hit 'options'.
Select 'send'.
Put in the phone #.
Hit 'send'.

It's gone. Your
grandchild is contacted !!
You're connected !!

WOW ! ! !
Kudo's from me . .
. & Hugs from ur grand kids

HINT: icon pictures & words
at top & bottom of your
phone screen

confusion can often be resolved
if you stop .....

& take a good look at the
icons (pictures) appearing at
the **top & bottom of the
screen**.

• **For example**:

You'll recall that in text
mode on your phone
screen, you have **Aa**Bb or
something similar. That
lets you know that the
letters you type will be
capitals & small letters.

If it looks like AaBB, then all
the letters will be capitals.

Notice which combination of
letters are **highlighted** and
that's what you'll get.

If you want to change this,
punch the * key.

- **Another example** about
pictures (icons) & words
on ur screen:

at the bottom, left of your
screen, you will see **'options'**
when you select that with

your very top left key, you will
get a drop-down menu that will
let you save your message into
'drafts'

As you begin practicing longer
messages, you can save into
'drafts' just to take a break &
go back to it later.

- Don't forget these
  important pictures &
  words on your screen
  that can guide you, or . . .

 can even perform the function
you're madly struggling to find.

In fact, if you're struggling.

Stop.
Take a deep breath.
Calmly look at your
screen & keys for something
you may have overlooked.   Have
fun!

OKAY.....
So, while you're doing so
great, let's try **one more,   just
for practice**:

How about: **"Please call
me as soon as you can."**

Text lingo:
"**Plz ph me asap**"

Now, you do it with steps

A, B, & **C**. Use the big
picture of the Key Pad on page
12 if that makes it easier.

A) - select 'text messaging'
        'create message'

B) - type in your message
        (Pls ph me asap)

C) - 'options' & 'send'

Excelllllent !!
You DiD it all by yourself!
The Grands R Great !!!

Now,

ABOUT
PUNCTUATION

For me, the biggest challenge is not the 'regular' alphabet letters and numbers, but figuring out where all the 'hidden' things are.

For example, on most phones, key pad 1 has most of the punctuation symbols that you use most often. So, let's look at punctuation.

PUNCTUATION:
 Most are on key pad 1

Key pad 1:
punch 1x = . (period)

punch 2x = @   ('at' symbol)

punch 3x =   , (comma)

punch 4x = - (dash)

punch 5x = ?   (question mark)

punch 6x = (exclamation mark)

punch 7x = :   (colon)

punch 8x = /   (forward slash)

If these are not in exactly the same place on your keypad, you will be able to find punctuation easily by pressing various keys.

But, so far, every phone I've looked at has most of them at the #1 key pad.

TRY THIS:
I found that fooling around with the key pad, finding hidden symbols & shortcuts is a great way to entertain myself while waiting for doctor appointments, or waiting to pick up those wonderful grand kids from school, rehearsals, or games.

Just anywhere you're stuck
waiting.

Some phones even have
symbols on the 'up' & 'down'
arrows on the key pad.

* It's a great stress reducer,
    too, because you're
    focused on something
    other than how long
    you've been waiting, how
    late things are running.

* I's also a fun thing to do if
    you end up with some
    free time and feel bored.

* It will entertain you and give
    you a great sense of

accomplishment. I
guarantee it! Because
I've done it.

Okay,
let's try a **message that
includes punctuation**.

Hmmm, how about
**"Hope to see you this
weekend!
Love, Grandpa"**

Text lingo:
"hp 2 c u ts wknd ! Luv,
Gpa"

& we'll add a **smiley face** at

the end just for fun! . .

hey!. . we're moving into advanced text messaging here. Not bad for ur fourth message !

You can do the letters on the key pad by now, so I'll just help you with the **punctuation & smiley face**.

 FYI: Text smiley faces are all sideways.

It's the only way to make them with the phone keys.
: D

Here we go:

A) - select
'text messaging'
'create message'

B) - type in your message:
hp 2 c u ts wknd !
After **wknd,**
use Key Pad 1 &
punch it 6x.

Luv, Gpa

If you want a **comma between**
Luv & Granpa,

then use Key Pad 1 & punch it
3x, or until you see the
comma.

For the **smiley face**:

Go to the #1 key pad & punch
    until the colon appears;

After the colon, type in a
    capital 'D'

: D

The kids use this face a lot.

    But, I'll show you another
way later! There are all sorts
of possibilities once you start
playing with this.

    Well, okay....**let's finish**

You've got the text entered:

'hp 2 c u ts wknd ! Luv, Gpa' : D

Now, do

C) - 'options',
enter phone #,
& 'send'

Another message done!
Ur doing gr8 ! ! !

Non-English letters

If you need to type a word that has an accent or some other symbol over one of the letters, you can usually find that letter by continuing to punch the key pad with the basic letter on it.

For example:
If you want an 'a' with an accent over it: **á**
Then, you would use Key Pad 2, just keep punching it until you see the á, and then stop.

In fact, you can find lots

of accented letters as well as other symbols, like math symbols & Greek letters this way. Just keep punching past the 'regular' letters and numbers. And, see what shows up. This is another thing to explore in your 'waiting room' time or while you're watching TV.

Now that ur a texter,

**PLEASE, please,
do THIS 4 me**

I want to hear your stories of how successful you were.
 Especially about your grandkids' reactions to your messages!

I know how much fun it can be and how absolutely fantastic I feel when I connect with my grandkids this way, and I would really love to hear your stories.

Send them to me at
        hhtp://www.vallipub.com
        Thanks ! : D

2. WORDS,
Emoticons (pictures),
ACRONYMS, & a few Phrases

WORDS: short versions of regular words lingo is sort of like an easy, code language.

Most words are short, 'sound alike versions of regularly spelled words.

This secret code is part of what makes it so much fun for kids and for us. It's a special lingo. (Are you old enough to remember pig-Latin?)

And, more than one word can have the same text lingo spelling. That means that which word it is depends on the context or what the message is about. But, this is not a problem. It's always obvious. Trust me.

* most words are short
        versions that leave out
        the vowels [a, e, i, o, u]

        Such as: sn = soon
        And, sometimes other
letters, too:
        bk = back

* vowels get included mostly
      when they sound like
      something else
      For example: good = gud

* acronyms, the first letter in a
series of words, are used a lot

i.e: an old acronym you might
      remember:
SWAK [sealed/sent with a kiss]

* letters are often combined
      with numbers to make
      words, as you've probably
      already noticed

for example: tonight = 2nite;
before = b4;   late = L8

HINT: This is a big help!
If you don't know the 'correct' text message spelling, then just wing it; kids can figure out about anything– that's how it all got started anyway with kids making up a short-hand as they went along messaging their friends.

EMOTICONS: symbols used to make pictures

*these are made from symbols found on your key pad

* usually used in various combination to make pictures

* used to convey emotions
        hence the name:
        emot = emotion
        icons = picture

* learning to combine these
        symbols to make
        emoticons may take a
        little playing around with
        the keypad–this will be
        fun

    You've already learned
how to do one—the smiley face

HINT play around with you
key pad while waiting in line or
for appointments. It's a good
time to discover ways to create
emoticons.
*FYI -kids, especially the
younger kids, make these sideways faces with all sort of
variation and additions - about
everything you can think of
given the key pad symbol range;
  happy, sad, frowning, with
hats....

        I just learned the basic,
        easy face. : D
        Now I can send a smile
with my message
        Good enough for now---

probably gud enuf 4ever, 4 me

But, I do know another way to make the face, and I can tell you I'm pretty proud of that fact!

Here's how the kids do it most of the time using punctuation symbols found on key pad #1

: -)   happy face with key pad 1 punctuation symbols

Here's How:

Use the *** key pad to change** your upper or lower, right or left (on the screen)

icon from AaBb to **T9Ab** (or whatever letter-number combination your phone shows). Just punch the * key pad until that combination comes up.

   Then, go to **Key Pad 1 and punch it 3x** quickly. Your smiley face will appear!

   To change your T9Ab back to the regular AaBb, hold Key Pad * down while punching Key Pad # until the desired AaBb combination appears. Changing from letters to numbers & back again is probably the most complex thing you'll ever have to do.

Tip: This way of making the smiley face is good practice for learning how to change the **AABb, 123, T9Aa,** options for using capitals and small letters.

The kids already know all these shortcuts, but for us grands, although we are grand in a multitude of ways, we have not necessarily achieved 'grandness' with the key pad.

But u have already sent messages. The rest is icing on the cake. Just playing around with the key pad.

So, now you can send messages AND you know 2 ways to make the happy face ! You're becoming a pro already !

**Ur ThR ! !   Ur a txtr !
Ez, wsn't it?**

**Go 4th   Txt   Hv fun
  Snd LuV   B LuVd** Here
are a few of the words in a
short dictionary to help you get
'into' the knack of text lingo.
After just a few messages, you
won't feel the need to look up
most words.

SHORT DICTIONARY

AN = N
AND = N
ANY = NE
ANYONE = NE1
ANYTHING = NETHNG
ARE = R

BACK = B of BK
BE = B
BEFORE = B4
BEING = BN
BORED = ZZZZZ
BOYFRIEND - B/F

CAN = CN
CHRISTMAS = XMAS
CROSSING = XNG

DOING = DOIN
DON'T = DNT

EASY = EZY
EXCELLENT = XLNT
EXTRA = XTRA

FOR = 4
FORWARD = FWD
FOUR = 4

GIVE = GIV
GREAT = GR8
GOOD = GUD

HATE = H8
HAVE = HV
HELLO = LO

IF = F
IS = S
IN = N

KISS = X

LATE = L8
LATER = L8R
LOVE = LUV
LUNCH = LCH

MEETING = MTNG
MESSAGE = MSG

NOTHING = NUTN

OFFICE = OFIS
OKAY = K

PEACE = PZ
PEOPLE = PPL
PLEASE = PLS
PHONE = PH
PROBABLY = PROLLY or PROB

SAYS = SEZ
SEE = C
SLEEPING = ZZZZ

THANK YOU = THNQ   or TU
THANKS = THX or TX
THE = D
THAT = DAT
TOMORROW = 2MORO
TONIGHT = 2NITE

WHEN = WEN
WEEK = WK
WERE = W
WHERE = W
WHY = Y?
WILL = WL
WITH = W

YOU = U or Q
YOUR = UR
YOU'RE = UR

PHRASES &
ACROMYMS

Always a pleasure = aap
Are you okay? = RUOK
Are you there = AYT

Big Grin = BG
Bye for now - B4N

Check your email = CYE

Dear Friend = DF
Dear Granddaughter = DGD
Dear Grandson = DGS
Fingers crossed = FC
Free to talk = F2T

Good night, sweet dreams =
    GNSD
Good try = GT

Hugs & Kisses = XOXOXO

I don't know - 404 (don't ask
    me the logic on this one)
I don't understand what you
    mean = ?
I have a question = ?
I have a question for you = ?4u

Laughing out loud = LOL
Long time no see - LTNS

Off to Bed = OTB
Over & Out = OO
Over my dead body = OMD

Parent watching = 9
Parents are watching = PAW
Praise the Lord = PTL

Think positive = T+

What's up? = ZUP

Yes I understand = YIU
You're the greatest! = YTG

3. WEB SITES: places to find lots more words, acronyms, phrases & emoticons

If you want to explore more words and how to make other emoticons, here are a few Web Sites that will help you get started.

HINT: Save these until you mastered the basic messaging.

http:/
/www.webopedia.com/quick_ref
/textmessageabbreviations.asp

At this site you can enter a text lingo word and it will give you the definition, or translation.

You can also click on any letter of the alphabet & go to the words starting with that letter in their text lingo dictionary.

They also have a link you can click on that tells you the meaning of a lot of different emoticons, and it shows you how to create them, also.

http://lingo2word.com/transla te.php

This site will translate your message of 'regular' words into text lingo and vice versa.

Pretty cool! Especially if you have a complicated or extra long message to send, or, more likely for me one I've received & can't fully translate–ones with acronyms & emoticons sometimes stump me.

http://www.netlingo.com/emailsh.cfm

This site offers a basic dictionary of acronyms, including letters & letter-number combinations that make up the many acronyms kids have created. Very helpful!

***You can also do a search for other web sites that have dictionaries or translations or emoticons.

CONNECT with your

GRAND KIDS !   Do it !
        Feel Gr8.   Luv thm.

: D   : D   : D

And, lastly....thx 4
learning how 2 txt. I
think it really adds love 2
the world. That it opens
communication with the
younger generations.
What could be more
important?   We all need
love & all our grand kids
need grandparents.

Notes & Phone Numbers

Made in the USA